Surrender, work, Live!

30 Days to Unbecome

Precious Bivings

Surrender, Work, Live!
30 Days to Unbecome™

Precious Bivings

Published by SWL, Publications
Greenville, SC

Printed in the United States of America

ISBN-13: 978-0692415689

ISBN-10: 0692415688

To you!

My beautiful, smart and funny one and only daughter,
Brettani. Thank you for teaching me all the many lessons
you've taught me.
You are my greatest accomplishment.
I love you!

Kisses from me to you!

Father God, I love you with my whole heart. I am so grateful for the sheer opportunity to serve you. Thank you for the countless blessings you continue to provide. Thank you for being a redeemer of time. Thank you for your grace and mercy. Thank you for giving me purpose. Without a shadow of doubt, I know I was born to inspire.

To you who are holding this book in your hands,
thank you!
This is your minute, your hour, your day, your week, your month, your year!
My hope for you is that you are inspired daily to create the life you were created to live!
Let's live life!

TABLE OF CONTENTS

One day at a time…..

You can only live life one day at a time. Yesterday has passed and tomorrow is not promised. Maximize today. Take each day, hour, minute, and second you are given to get one more step closer to living your best life

Each day that you Unbecome, you are one more step closer to creating the life you want to live!

Unbecome™
Surrender, Work, Live!

There are three steps to the Unbecome process: surrender, work and live!

Surrender: This means to cease resistance. Stop fighting the process of life. Yield to whatever is coming and allow it to pass by you. Don't try to fight it. If you feel hurt, allow yourself to be present in it and allow the feeling to pass. Going through life holding on to everything that comes your way is how you get stuck! Surrender. Throw your hands up. Let it go.

Work: Work, by definition, means to actively involve mental or physical effort done in order to achieve a purpose or result. The work that I'm referring to is the "f" word everybody wants to *talk* about but is not actually willing to *do:* forgiveness! Often, we're afraid to forgive because we think that in forgiving, we give permission to be hurt and mishandled. That's not true. Forgiveness actually sets you free!

Live: To live means to have an exciting or fulfilling life. It doesn't mean to just flow through life like a bump on a log. You have to go and get life! Living is being brave, taking a chance and making it happen!

Make every day count! Unbecome!

Day 1 to Unbecome

Procrastination
(The robber of time)

So you decided to wait until tomorrow...or Monday...or Friday? What the heck are you waiting for? There is no time like the present. You are as you have been because you haven't made a move. The funny thing is that you're hoping things change. Wake up! Nothing will change until you make the change happen. Time is waiting for no one. In fact, time, unlike money, can never be earned again once it's spent. Get to it and make it happen. When? Today!

Surrender:
Let go of the idea that you'll get it done another day.
Work:
Forgive yourself for wasting time that you now know can never be earned again.
Live!
Make the move today! Every day going forward, cherish the time you have.

Day 2 to Unbecome

Fear
(But what if...?)

And I ask you, "What if?" What if you are as great as you are afraid to be? What if some people like you and some people don't? What if you fail, and what if you don't? Fear is often referred to as *false evidence appearing real.* Allow fear to motivate you, not stagnate you! Do it afraid! Now that you know better, do better! No longer do you have the excuse of "what if?" Now, you have the responsibility to take another step to create the life you were created to live!

Surrender:
Let go of the idea of "what if?"
Work:
Forgive yourself for being afraid and allowing fear to rule you.
Live!
Put fear in its proper place. Face it and move forward!

Day 3 to Unbecome

Impatience
(I want what I want now!)

I've been there. In fact, some days, I'm still there. Waiting can be a hard thing to do if all you're doing is waiting. There is work to do when you're waiting. Like what? Whatever you can do. While you're waiting for an answer, start working on something else. While you're waiting for someone to show up, read, make a phone call, pray or relax. While you're waiting for a need or for something you want, decide to be there for someone until it's your turn to receive.

More than anything, don't cause yourself to become stressed. Take a deep breath and work while you wait. Relax. There are so many benefits to having patience, like learning to master or impulses and responses, allowing us to reflect before we respond.

Surrender:
Let go of the idea that you're waiting is in vain.
Work:
Forgive yourself for stressing your mind, body and soul because you had to wait.
Live!
Decide ahead of time to work while you wait so that you can make the most of every opportunity, including waiting!

Day 4 to Unbecome

Jealousy
(It should have been me!)

Being jealous has so much to do with fear, it's not even funny. Jealousy is an inner fear that there isn't enough. Jealousy is a fear of lack. The awesome thing about God is that He is almighty. There is more than enough to go around. Your soul has its own audience, assignments and responsibilities. Your plate is so full that if you'd just focus on yourself, there would be no room for the fear of there not being enough for you.

Surrender:
Let go of the idea that there isn't enough. There is plenty with your name on it!

Work:
Forgive yourself for taking your focus away from what's important – you!

Live!
Congratulate, encourage, motivate and celebrate those who you've been jealous of. Take the focus off of them and mind your business so that you can create the life you want to live!

Day 5 to Unbecome

Negative Self-Talk
(Stinking Thinking)

The most important conversation that you will ever have is the one you have with yourself. How you talk to yourself matters. If you are consistently speaking negatively to yourself, there is no way for you to be or do any better than where you are. Your success depends on how you speak to yourself. In order to achieve the goals you've set for yourself, start with talking positively to and about yourself. Replace "I can't" with "I can" and "I will." Encourage yourself. Speak life to yourself. Speak love to yourself.

Surrender:
Let go of your stinking thinking and negative self-talk.
Work:
Look in the mirror. Take a deep breath and ask yourself for forgiveness for the way you spoke and thought about yourself.
Live!
Every day, starting today, look in the mirror and say three positive statements about yourself.

Day 6 to Unbecome

Inauthenticity
(Not Being You)

Never ask for permission to be you. Just be you. Yes, there will be people who don't like who you are. There are also people who don't like who you're pretending to be. Either way, that's not your problem. You are missing out on authentic, productive and beneficial relationships because who you're pretending to be is attracting all the wrong people. You are more than good enough. Who you truly are matters.

Surrender:
Let go of the idea that the real you is not good enough.
Work:
Forgive yourself for not being you.
Live!
Introduce the world to the real you!

Day 7 to Unbecome

Self-Doubt
(I don't trust myself!)

I've been there and had to live with the regret of not trusting myself. How do we get to a place of self-doubt or not trusting ourselves? We get there by not being true to ourselves, not protecting ourselves or loving ourselves in a way that produces or promotes trust. It's no different than when you love someone or someone loves you. The trust is built by actions and decisions that are conducive to the love you say that you have for others. You are no different to yourself. It is important to build the type of relationship with yourself that involves love, trust and honor. Make decisions for yourself that you are proud of. That alone will build your confidence in trusting you!

Surrender:
Let go of the idea that how you treat yourself doesn't matter.
Work:
Forgive yourself for not putting you first.
Live!
Today is the day that you begin to make decisions that are for your best interest and well-being!

Day 8 to Unbecome

Distraction
(I keep losing my focus!)

Stop allowing yourself to be distracted (yes, I said allowing yourself). You own the rights to your own thoughts. I know this may be hard to believe, but you have the power to choose your thoughts like you choose when and where you spend your money. Be selective. Be conscious. When you find yourself distracted by thoughts, people or things, use your power to snap out of it and refocus yourself. It takes practice. You have the power to be distraction free.

Surrender:
Let go of the idea that you can't control your thoughts.
Work:
Forgive yourself and others for the distractions.
Live!
Start practicing choosing your thoughts and exercising your own power over your own thoughts!

Day 9 to Unbecome

Expectation
(The way I believe it should be)

The problem with expectations is that at the root of an expectation is often an assumption. This is coupled with how we think or believe something should be, which often results in a big disappointment or letdown. Having an assumed expectation doesn't change the outcome; it only adds pressure. Release your expectation by being unconditional. Decide from the start how you will respond no matter the outcome. The benefits of releasing expectations are not just for you but for the people you are holding to a certain expectation. Free yourself from the burden of holding an expectation and free others to just be!

Surrender:
Let go of the idea that holding an expectation will change the outcome.
Work:
Forgive yourself for holding expectations and ask for forgiveness for holding others to your expectation if needed.
Live!
Today, walk in the freedom of being expectation-free!

Day 10 to Unbecome

Being the Victim
(Look at what they did to me!)

The problem with being the victim is that you miss the opportunity to take ownership of yourself and what is happening with you. You are not a victim; you are a victor. Stop walking around, talking about what someone else did to you, and decide to take ownership of the only person you can control – you. Pointing the finger only delays the growing process and puts you at risk of a replay. Decide to take ownership of yourself. You can't control how someone else treats you, but what you can control is how you respond.

Surrender:
Let go of the idea that you have no control over what happens to you.
Work:
Forgive yourself for deciding to be a victim instead of a victor.
Live!
Today, decide that no matter what happens, you will take ownership of yourself and be victorious – not a victim.

Day 11 to Unbecome

Entitlement
(The world owes me!)

Stop waiting around for someone to rescue you. No one but yourself owes you. Having an attitude of entitlement says that you deserve something you haven't worked for. Feeling entitled will only allow you to receive what others think you deserve. Instead of being entitled, be empowered and create the life you were created to live!

Surrender:
Let go of the idea that the world owes you.
Work:
Forgive yourself for being entitled instead of empowered.
Live!
Today, wait for no one. Go make it happen!

Day 12 to Unbecome

Being Numb
(Feelings suck!)

So, you've been hurt before, maybe even many times. You've decided not to feel in order to avoid being hurt again. I see. The problem with being numb is that it doesn't allow you to heal. Being numb keeps you stuck in the very same feeling you're doing your best to avoid. I can't promise you that you'll never be hurt again. What I can promise is that if you allow yourself to feel and heal, you will be so much better for it.

Surrender:
Let go of the false protection of being numb to your feelings.
Work:
Forgive yourself for not allowing yourself to feel.
Live!
From today going forward, decide to acknowledge your feelings by writing them in your journal daily.

Day 13 to Unbecome

Narrow-minded
(I only think one way)

There is so much freedom in being open-minded. You get to explore, grow and decide for yourself. Being open-minded doesn't mean that you believe everything that you hear or see. It means: "I believe what I believe, but I'm also interested in learning more." Trust me – there is more than one way to see the world. Being narrow-minded boxes you into one way. Be open to explore, grow and see!

Surrender:
Let go of the idea that there is only one way.
Work:
Forgive yourself for not being open to explore and grow.
Live!
Make a decision today to be open to a different way.

Day 14 to Unbecome

Resistance
(I'm still fighting)

There used to be a time when you felt like you had to fight against everything. Today is not that day. Stop fighting the process. Instead, go with the flow of the process that is created to make you a better person. When you stop fighting and surrender, everything comes together. There is a time for everything. Today, relax and breathe.

Surrender:
Let go of the idea that you have to fight against everything.
Work:
Forgive yourself for using energy to fight what's best for you.
Live!
Today, use your energy toward being creative versus resistant.

Day 15 to Unbecome

Past Hurts
(It's the song that never ends)

Everyone has experienced hurt on some level. You are not alone. The way to recover from past hurt is to forgive it. You're probably saying, "Easier said than done." I'm saying, "Easier to forgive than to live in the hurt of your past." Instead, live in the freedom of forgiving your past so that you can move forward with creating your best life!

Surrender:
Let go of the idea that holding onto your past hurt somehow makes you a better person.
Work:
Forgive yourself for holding onto something that doesn't serve you!
Live!
Starting today, be a peace with your past and create an even better present and future.

Day 16 to Unbecome

Bitterness
(I'm not ready to forgive)

Bitterness is what happens when you choose not to forgive. Bitterness is the result of not letting go of hurt. The problem with bitterness is that it contaminates your perspective. It blocks you from enjoying life and those that you love. Choose to be better, not bitter.

Surrender:
Let go of that bad taste in your mouth when you think of someone or a situation.
Work:
Forgive yourself for allowing bitterness to take root.
Live!
Forgive instantaneously.

Day 17 to Unbecome

Shame
(I'm a bad person)

There is a difference between shame and guilt. Guilt is the feeling that is often associated with remorse and responsibility for an undesired action and allows you to have empathy toward the outcome of what you've done. Shame makes you feel bad about yourself versus what you've done. Shame is your way of covering up and judging yourself in a negative light. Stop shaming yourself and correct the behavior you wish to change.

Surrender:
Let go of the idea that shame is a benefactor to your growth.
Work:
Forgive yourself for living in shame and forgive those who have shamed you.
Live!
Today, decide to uncover shame by telling the truth and making the necessary changes.

Day 18 to Unbecome

A Bad Day
(Nobody knows, the trouble)

Sometimes, it's just one of those days where nothing seems to go your way. Everything that could go wrong does. What you should know is that even in the worst conditions, having a positive perspective and outlook won't change the situation but will change your experience of the situation. Seeing the glass half full instead of half empty allows for you to get the best out of the worst. Think big and begin in gratitude!

Surrender:
Let go of the idea that a bad day can't get better.
Work:
Forgive the contributors of the bad day.
Live!
Today, decide to have a positive outlook and a great day no matter what.

Day 19 to Unbecome

Thinking Small
(I like playing it safe)

There is nothing you can't do. It's truly up to you. Do something big! What seems big for you may not be big for someone else, and that's okay. You know what big looks like for you. Big may be walking up to a stranger and initiating a conversation. Or big may be walking away from your 9 to 5 to pursue your purpose. Today is your day!

Think big!

Surrender:
Let go of being safe and playing it small.
Work:
Forgive yourself for allowing fear to stop you!
Live!
Today, commit to taking at least one step toward your best self!

Day 20 to Unbecome

Dishonesty
(Everybody lies about something, right?)

I've heard it said before that we all lie about something. From hair extensions to implants and white lies to flat-out perjury, the bottom line is that not living in the truth repels opportunities and authentic relationships. Not to mention, you lose trust with the most important person in your life – you. Your word matters. Live the truth.

Surrender:
Let go of the idea that being dishonest is a benefit.
Work:
Forgive yourself for sewing distrust with yourself and others.
Live!
When you get the urge to exaggerate or lie, pause and decide to tell the truth.

Day 21 to Unbecome

Being Late or Delinquent
(I'm only five minutes late.)

Time is a precious commodity. Unlike money, you can't get time back. Once it's gone, it's gone. I once read that a guy took reading material every time he attended a meeting so that if the meeting started late, his time would not be wasted. Stealing time from other people by showing up late is a big deal because it's something you can't replace. Plus, it shows a lack of respect toward the other person. Make a conscious effort to show up early so that you are never late.

Remember, time is the most precious resource we all have.

Surrender:
Let go of the idea that being late is not important.
Work:
Ask for forgiveness and forgive yourself for robbing others of their time.
Live!
Today, make a conscious effort to be a good steward of the time you share with others as well as the time you spend alone.

Day 22 to Unbecome

Drama
(But you didn't hear that from me)

Drama can be so addictive. We watch it on reality television, we listen to it in music and we spread it through conversations. What's so addictive about drama? Maybe it's the false sense of relief from our own drama. Drama is a tremendous waste of time and energy. If we're not careful, it very quickly puts us smack dead in the middle and causes us to lose focus on what's really important – your own business!

Surrender:
Let go of the idea that you need drama in order to make life interesting.
Work:
Forgive yourself for participating in drama.
Live!
Today, recognize and dismiss the drama so that you can continue to create your own best life!

Day 23 to Unbecome

Voiceless
(Can you hear me now?)

Being heard can sometimes seem difficult, especially if you have made a practice of standing in the shadows, hearing from others and telling yourself that what you have to say isn't so important. You have a right to be heard. What you have to say does matter. The first person it has to matter to is yourself. Speaking up for yourself ensures that your needs are met and that you are properly understood. What you think, feel and say matters.

Surrender:
Let go of the idea that what you have to say isn't important.
Work:
Forgive yourself for not regarding yourself with total honor.
Live!
Today, backing down is not an option. Speak up for yourself!

Day 24 to Unbecome

Being Unprepared
(I'm not ready!)

Successful people are prepared. The more prepared you are, the better the outcome is of any situation. Life has its way of throwing you a surprise party. Prepare for what you can so that you can use time and energy to handle those unexpected situations. The disadvantage to not being prepared is that you lose time, energy and money. You will save more by preparing rather than paying the cost for convenience. Prepare so that you don't have to live in a state of paranoia. Being prepared means that you have what you need when you need it.

Surrender:
Let go of the idea that you don't have time to prepare.
Work:
Forgive yourself for not taking the time to prepare.
Live!
Today, take the time to prepare and reap the benefits!

Day 25 to Unbecome

Rejection
(I don't like to be told no)

You're not going to be everybody's cup of tea. And guess what? That's perfectly okay. Although being rejected can hurt, there are benefits. Sometimes, rejection comes as a sign that the situation is not best suited for you, even when you really want it to be. Sometimes, rejection comes as a sign that self-improvement is needed. Be willing to acknowledge how you feel and grow from the experience. Deciding to clam up and never initiate something because of your fear of rejection only robs you of new, fresh opportunities and relationships.

Surrender:
Let go of the idea that rejection means you're not good enough.
Work:
Forgive yourself for allowing the fear of rejection to rob you of opportunities and new relationships.
Live!
Today, live life as if rejection doesn't exist.

Day 26 to Unbecome

Desperation
(I need and have to have you)

When you feel desperate, it causes you to make decisions that you wouldn't ordinarily make. Take a look at the root of desperation; it is often associated with low self-worth. Know that you have everything you need inside of you. No one outside of you can fill that void but God. You are more than enough.

Surrender:
Let go of the idea that you are not worthy of time and love.
Work:
Forgive yourself for ever expecting that someone outside of yourself will save you.
Live!
Today, should you feel the need to reach outside of yourself, grab your courage and pull from inside of you everything that you need.

Day 27 to Unbecome

Disappointment
(The letdown)

You've heard it said before that when life hands you lemons, make lemonade, right? That's not just a cute cliché but a way to overcome disappointment. The way to defeat disappointment is persistence. Don't give up! If Michael Jordan would have given up when he was cut from his high school basketball team, he would have never met his greatness. Some of our greatest life achievers faced great disappointment. The secret is that they never gave up! When you see disappointment, get ready to flex your muscles and persevere!

Surrender:
Let go of the idea that disappointment means defeat.
Work:
Forgive yourself for allowing disappointment to defeat you.
Live!
Today, persevere by facing disappointment with your head held high!

Day 28 to Unbecome

Not Forgiving
(I'm still living in the past)

When we choose not to forgive others, we are choosing to hold on to the hurt and pain associated with the action and behavior of a person. Not forgiving causes additional hurt, pain, bitterness and even depression. Forgiveness opens doors and allows one to extend grace. When battling with whether or not you should forgive, consider the weight you are sure to carry if you choose not to forgive.

Surrender:
Let go of the idea that choosing not to forgive someone is teaching them a lesson.
Work:
Forgive yourself for choosing not to release pain and hurt by forgiving. Then, forgive others.
Live!
Today, let go and forgive everyone for everything!

Day 29 to Unbecome

Irresponsibility
(It's not my fault!)

It's easy to give up responsibility. Blaming others is often more comfortable than taking ownership. Own your stuff. In order to improve your life, you must first take responsibility of your life. The day of blaming your parents, situations, or circumstances for the outcome of your life has expired. The responsibility of your life is your own.

Surrender:
Let go of the idea that someone else is to blame for the condition of your life outside of you.
Work:
Forgive yourself for not taking responsibility for your life and blaming others.
Live!
Today, take ownership your life and make decisions that will create the life you were meant to live!

Day 30 to Unbecome

Low Self-Esteem
(I haven't learned how special I am)

Having low self-esteem causes you to be pretentious, judgmental and critical of other people. Build your self-esteem by being authentic and loving yourself, not "the you" after you've fixed this or lost that but right where you are. Give yourself permission to make mistakes and own your actions. You can't bring to yourself what you don't already have inside. Create the person that you were created to be!

Surrender:
Let go of the idea that you aren't good enough.
Work:
Forgive yourself for not believing in yourself.
Live!
Today, look in the mirror and tell yourself:
_____your name here_____, you are more than enough!

About Precious Bivings

Precious Bivings is a results-driven life coach, empowerment speaker and executive workshop facilitator who is committed to helping you develop, create and implement your ideal life by assisting you in staying focused, challenged and motivated personally and professionally! As an empowerment speaker and workshop facilitator, she has developed a process that is driven to help you live your best!

She is CEO and Founder of Brettani's Heritage Life Recovery Organization.

Let's get connected!

Facebook: Precious Bivings / Precious Bivings, The Life Speaker
Facebook: Brettani's Heritage, A Life Recovery Organization
Twitter: @preciousbivings
Web: www.preciousbivings.com
Web: www.brettanisheritage.org

Made in the USA
Middletown, DE
16 August 2023

36844432R00024